SUMMARY

Review & Analysis of
Jared Diamond's Book

Collapse

BusinessNews Publishing

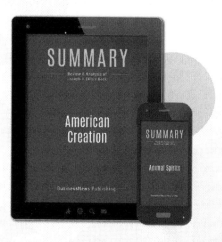

BOOK PRESENTATION: *COLLAPSE* BY JARED DIAMOND

BOOK ABSTRACT

In *Collapse*, Jared Diamond argues that present global resource consumption trends are not sustainable. Throughout history, civilizations have collapsed or declined, in no small measure, because their populations have undermined the ecological niches upon which their existence depends. Diamond believes that a complex set of factors, such as environmental resilience (or fragility), social flexibility, larger global trends and even pure luck, combine in unpredictable ways to influence whether societies fail or succeed.

Studying how past civilizations have met, or failed to meet, environmental challenges may prove crucial in averting future global calamities. In the past, when a civilization failed, its impact was usually localized. But in today's interconnected world, a failure in one part of the globe will have wide repercussions that have the potential to affect all mankind. This should cause us great concern, but by acknowledging the serious challenges we face, we may yet be able to avoid some of the worst catastrophes that might await us otherwise.

ABOUT THE AUTHOR

Jared Diamond teaches geography at the University of California and is the Pulitzer Prize winning author of *Guns, Germs, and Steel.* One of the most distinguished experts in the field of evolutionary biology, Diamond's work draws interest and acclaim from both academics and the general public. He has written more than 200 articles for magazines such as *Discover, Nature* and *Geo*, and his work has proven highly influential in informing public discourse on a range of environmental and social issues.

SUMMARY OF *COLLAPSE* (JARED DIAMOND)

COLLAPSES PAST AND PRESENT

The collapses of societies tend to display recurrent themes or patterns. Population growth, for example, tends to encourage intensified methods of agricultural production. However, unsustainable agricultural practices invariably lead to ecological damage, consequently leading to food shortages, starvation, wars and civil unrest. Eventually, a society's population is decreased through these factors, as well as the society's complexity, which gave rise to the unsustainable population excesses in the first place. Thus, many writers draw analogies between the life span of human beings and the life span of civilizations – they speak of the birth, growth, decline and death of societies – but in actuality, most societies collapse rather suddenly compared to the extended senescence that attends human aging.

Ecocide, or ecological suicide, is an issue that appears to be eclipsing nuclear holocaust as the biggest threat to global civilization. Small-scale ecological catastrophes have already taken place in Somalia, Rwanda and other Third World countries. The environmental threats we face today are the same as those that have undermined previous human societies. Therefore, studying how past societies handled ecological challenges are vital if we are to avert the numerous threats that are virtually certain to become critical over the next several decades.

FIVE-POINT FRAMEWORK

It isn't possible to blame a society's collapse solely on environmental damage – there are always other factors. However, there is a five-point framework for attempting to describe any putative collapse. They are:

1. Environmental Damage
2. Climate Change
3. Hostile Neighbors
4. Friendly Trading Partners
5. A Society's Response to Environmental Challenges

The first four may or may not prove decisive in a society's collapse, but the fifth factor always proves significant.

Environmental damage will depend not just on a native population, but also on the inherent fragility or resilience of a given environment. Historically, at least, climate change has been another factor that was beyond a population's ability to control

The presence or absence of hostile neighbors is another factor that can tip the balance of a society succeeding or failing. Often, a society will be able to hold off its enemies when it is strong, but succumb when it is weakened for environmental reasons. "Hence, collapses for ecological reasons often masquerade as military defeats."

Friendly trading partners can also play a huge role in whether a given society meets its challenges. For instance, most societies depend heavily on trading partners to secure vital resources, but a weakened trading partner can greatly weaken one's own society.

The fifth factor, how a society chooses to respond to environmental challenges, depends on a civilization's economic and political institutions, along with its cultural values. Societies can fail to recognize such challenges, ignore them, adopt futile or counterproductive responses, or, on occasion, succeed in meeting environmental challenges through conservation and technological and other innovative solutions.

STUDYING COLLAPSES SCIENTIFICALLY

Can one study the collapse of civilizations scientifically? "After all, most people assume science is a body of knowledge acquired by performing controlled and replicable experiments." In some fields however - population biology, astronomy and geology, for instance - controlled experiments are unfeasible and other rigorous methods are required.

"A frequent solution is to apply what is termed the 'comparative method' or the 'natural experiment' – i.e., to compare natural situations differing with respect to the variable of interest." In other words, it is possible to rate societies on a number of variables - deforestation, rainfall, soil fertility, etc., - and then tease out by statistical analysis what particular variables contributed to success or failure, leading to insights and knowledge useful for meeting our own environmental challenges.

UNDER MONTANA'S BIG SKY

Montana is one of America's largest states, but it is also among the least populous. It appears to be one of the most unspoiled landscapes in the United States. Yet, Montana's environmental problems include almost all of the factors that undermined pre-industrial societies of the past. These include toxic waste, biodiversity loss, climate change and introduced pests. The problems Montana faces are not insurmountable, but they do illustrate the complexity of environmental issues and the inevitable tradeoffs between civilization and ecological damage.

Montana's mining industry, for instance, is a case in point. Civilization simply cannot subsist without exploiting natural resources like coal, zinc and copper, to say nothing of cutting down forests for timber and diverting water sources for crop irrigation and the like. Though some forms of mining are more environmentally friendly than others, there is simply no way to avoid detrimental environmental impacts from mining, such as toxic run off. That's because in the case of many precious metals essential for modern conveniences, tons of raw material must be unearthed to yield even a few ounces of a vital metal.

Complicating matters is that fact that, historically, privately-owned companies are in the business of making a profit for their shareholders, so they have a fiduciary duty to maximize profits and minimize costs associated with cleanups. Complicating matters even further, many of Montana's present toxic waste problems are due to mining operations that ceased to exist decades ago. The public, naturally, is usually reluctant to shoulder higher taxes to pay for handling toxic waste problems, particularly if they are out of sight or not immediately imminent. This kind of thinking reflects the "tragedy of the commons" − if a danger looks remote, everyone assumes it must be someone else's responsibility.

Compounding this problem is the fact that most of Montana's citizens are conservatives, fiercely independent types who are deeply suspicious of governmental oversight or intervention to address ecological matters. As a result, zoning laws governing private property and development are virtually non-existent, hampering progress in addressing many of Montana's ecological challenges, which include: soil erosion, salinization (too much salt in the soil) and a general decline in agricultural efficiency.

Thus, Montana's ecological problems are becoming economic problems. One obvious affect of this is that an increasing amount of farmland is being converted for other uses, especially the development of summer homes for out-of-state residents. This has led to a substantial drop in Montana's per-capita income (out-of-state residents pay less of their share in state taxes), and an increasing share of Montana's income comes from out-of-state transfers – Social Security, Medicare, Agricultural subsidies, etc. "If Montana were an isolated island, as Easter Island in the Pacific Ocean was in Polynesian times before European arrival, its present First World economy would already have collapsed." But because Montana is not isolated - nor is the United States - it is not in imminent danger of collapse. Still, Montana's ecologically induced economic challenges may indicate some of the broad trends we should be concerned about heading into the future.

PAST SOCIETIES: TWILIGHT AT EASTER

Easter Island is home to some of the most unusual and mysterious artifacts the world has ever known. Who were the inhabitants of the lush island paradise who carved the gigantic stone figures that dot the landscape of their remote volcanic island? How did the ancestors of the isolated and primitive Polynesians, discovered by Dutch explorer Jacob Roggeveen, manage to erect such enormous figures? Perhaps we will never be able to entirely answer these questions, but one thing is clear, all the best biological and forensic evidence suggests Easter Island underwent a catastrophic deforestation some time around the 1400 A.D, roughly 600 years after the first inhabitants arrived (900 A.D)

In fact, the deforestation picture for Easter Island is the most extreme example anywhere in the Pacific, or even the world. The implications of deforestation for Easter Island's inhabitants were severe: lack of wood meant the natives could no longer build the canoes needed to fish or travel to the islands of trading partners, there was no wood fuel to burn during the winter and there was no supply of the raw materials to construct basic shelters. Deforestation also had other impacts, especially soil erosion leading to drastic decreases in agricultural output. The immediate consequences were grim indeed: starvation, a sharp decline in population and even a descent into cannibalism.

By the time Captain Cook had arrived at the island in 1774, he could describe the remaining inhabitants as "small, lean, timid, and miserable." What had taken place was a complete breakdown on the political, moral and religious ideologies. The toppled and desecrated statues that so capture our imagination almost certainly represent evidence of a revolt by the masses against their governing political and religious elites (not at all dissimilar to the toppling of Stalin's statue in Russia or Ceausescu's in Romania when Communism failed). Although some observers contend that European visitors prior to Roggeveen's could have played a role in Easter Island's ecological calamity, the available evidence does not support that conclusion. Instead, it appears that the inhabitants of Easter Island were living in one of the most fragile ecological environments, one inherently at risk for deforestation. In other words, Easter Island natives were not unusually ecologically inconsiderate as much as they were unlucky.

Actually, the inhabitants of Easter Island were doubly unfortunate – when their environment collapsed they had nowhere else to go. The example of Easter Island should be chillingly obvious; thanks to globalization, we on planet earth are as interconnected and isolated as the clans of Easter Island. Their fate may serve as a metaphor for a potential worst-case scenario awaiting us.

THE ANCIENT ONES: THE ANASAZI

The site of the ecological collapse closest to home, for Americans anyway, is that of the Anasazi societies in New Mexico. Although the Anasazi did not represent a huge civilization in terms of population, as the Maya did in South America, they did erect some of the largest and tallest buildings in North America until the 1880s.

The Anasazi do not represent the collapse of a single society, but rather a series of them. Like most collapses, no single factor can account for the demise of the Anasazi, but a fragile environment, marginal for agriculture, certainly looms as one of the most important. Nevertheless, the intersection of climate change, population problems, environmental damage and warfare with competing tribes illustrates just how quickly societies can collapse after attaining peak population numbers and power.

The Southwestern corner of North America has always presented a challenge to its inhabitants – namely, how to obtain adequate water in an environment with a generally low and unpredictable rainfall. All of the solutions to this problem found by the Anasazi posed a similar risk: that several years of adequate rainfall and effective water management would result in increased population growth that could not be sustained, particularly when a series of years with inadequate rainfall occurred.

Problems of water management proved particularly acute for the inhabitants of Chaco Canyon, the site of Pueblo settlements that were several stories high. Originally, the Chaco Canyon region seemed like an oasis in the desert, but archeological evidence indicates that Anasazi irrigation methods ultimately exacerbated their water management problems and their growing population quickly led to complete deforestation.

Despite these two major environmental problems, the Anasazi population managed to increase in spurts so long as climate conditions were favorable – i.e., many wet years in a row. However, an increasingly dense population could no longer support itself, particularly in years of decreased rainfall. Eventually, Chaco became a black hole where goods were imported from outside settlements, but which produced no exports by itself.

By this time, Chaco had become a mini-empire with a well-fed elite and a barely-subsisting peasantry. Inevitably, as resource scarcity increased, so did strife. Archeological evidence indicates that warfare and civil unrest became intense, including signs of cannibalism. The final blow appears to have been a prolonged drought that led to the abandonment of Chaco Canyon by the Anasazi. If we can draw a lesson from the Anasazi it is this: we can get away with waste when times are good, but when conditions fluctuate, we may be in for trouble.

THE MAYA COLLAPSES

The ruins of Mayan temples in Mexico's Yucatan Peninsula and parts of Central America have captured the imagination of millions of tourists. Though Mayan civilization collapsed more than 1,000 years ago, in their time, they were the New World's most advanced culture and the only Native American society with extensive written records.

The existence of decipherable texts means that anthropologists can reconstruct Mayan history to a far greater extent than that of the Anasazi or inhabitants of Easter Island. Contrary to popular belief, Mayan civilization did not spring up in a conventional tropical rainforest, but rather in a habitat called a "seasonal tropical rain forest," meaning there were alternating wet and dry periods within a typical year. Partly as a result of this, and partly as a result of porous sponge-like limestone terrain, the Mayans experience water management problems. This left many Mayan settlements vulnerable to prolonged droughts.

The Mayan's reliance on slash and burn agricultural techniques, corn-based agriculture (a crop that is low in protein) and a humid climate, which made food storage difficult, contributed to food supply problems. And food supply problems contributed to the fact that Mayan society "remained divided among small kingdoms that were perpetually at war with each other." This led to "power cycling" as individual cities grew in power, declined, got conquered and then rose again.

How did Mayan civilization eventually collapse? Anthropologists vigorously disagree among themselves, but some factors stand out. Population growth almost certainly outstripped available food resources, which precipitated deforestation, which may have been exacerbated by drought. Increased fighting among the Mayans for scarce resources would have amplified these factors (populations mobilized for warfare are usually less efficient agriculturally). It seems, also, that the kings and nobles failed to recognize and solve the obvious problems that were undermining their societies, focusing instead on short-term concerns such as enriching themselves and waging war. The Mayan elite, much like the elites of Easter Island and the Anasazi – or like the CEOs of many American companies in 21st century – were bent on extravaganza as their societies foundered.

OPPOSITE PATHS TO SUCCESS

Not all societies that encounter environmental problems are doomed to collapse. Even societies with limited space and relatively high population densities can discover optimal approaches of environmental management. In general, there are two basic approaches to environmental management: a "top-down" approach and a "bottom-up" approach.

In a bottom-up approach, everyone is immediately affected by environmental decisions, everyone realizes that they will benefit if they and their neighbors adopt sound environmental measures. Bottom-up management, then, is when local people work together to solve their own problems.

The top-down approach, on the other hand, is usually associated with large societies with centralized political organizations. For instance, in larger societies, a farmer in one region may be unfamiliar with ecological problems in another region, so the need arises for a centralized authority to take a general overview of environmental challenges for the society as a whole. In sum, bottom-up approaches are usually best suited to small societies and the top-down for larger societies, though medium-sized societies may find that neither of these two approaches suits them alone. In particular, bottom-up approaches to serious deforestation and environmental challenges have proven effective in New Guinea, while top-down approaches proved successful for comparable problems in Japan.

WHY JAPAN SUCCEEDED

A visitor to Japan in the middle of the 17th century might have predicted the country was heading for a collapse triggered by catastrophic deforestation, but Japan was able to surmount its challenges. Japan, unlike the Mayan, the Anasazi or the inhabitants of Easter Island, is fortunate in having a robust environment. For instance, Japan has rapid rates of tree re-growth thanks to abundant rainfall, high fallout from volcanic ash helps restore soil fertility and Japan possess sources of abundant seafood, which relieves pressure on forests as a source of protein.

Social factors also contributed to Japan's success in solving its environmental problems. For example, because peasants controlled their own land and could pass their land onto their heirs, Japan's resources were in the hands of people who had a vested interest in taking the longer view environmentally. Similarly, the Japanese elite, because they presided over an isolated and homogenous society, felt fewer internal and external threats than their Mayan counterparts say, thus encouraging them to take an extended view of resource conservation.

MALTHUS IN AFRICA

The recent genocide in Rwanda represents one of the most tragic events of the late 20th century. Although most Westerners view the violence between the Hutus and Tutsis as ethnically and religiously motivated, this is only part of the story and it overlooks an essential ecological dimension. Although the two ethnic groups have a complex and troubled political history, it is also true that the land they share is desperately overpopulated and agriculturally stressed and unproductive. As a result, Rwanda, like other parts of Africa, periodically faces tragic dilemmas of Malthusian proportions.

The English economist Thomas Malthus is best known for his controversial contention that while food supplies tend to increase arithmetically, populations tend to increase exponentially. As a result, population growth always outstrips the available food supplies, absent epidemics, natural disasters and the like. As early as 1984, many observers began to sense that Rwanda was an ecological disaster waiting to happen. Soil erosion coupled with deforestation, poor agricultural practices and high population density almost assured that a textbook calamity of Malthusian proportions was ready to explode. Unfortunately, many Rwandans themselves have come to believe that periodic genocides are necessary to get "population numbers into line with the available land resources." In short, what may appear to be ethnically motivated genocide is actually driven by ecological factors.

ONE ISLAND, TWO PEOPLES: THE DOMINICAN REPUBLIC AND HAITI

The Dominican Republican and Haiti are two countries that share a single island. Yet, the Dominican Republic has managed to meet its ecological challenges far more successfully while Haiti is something of an ecological nightmare. What accounts for such differing outcomes? Both are poor countries that share a history of European colonialism and American occupation. Some environmental differences do exist, but much of the explanation of why The Dominican Republic has succeeded and Haiti has fallen behind has to do with issues of attitudes, self-identity, institutions and leadership. This should put to rest any extreme version of "environmental determinism," or the idea that human agency cannot make a difference in surmounting ecological challenges.

This is not to say that ecological differences are not a factor in the diverging outcomes of Haiti and the Dominican Republic. Indeed, the Dominican portion of the island receives greater rainfall, supporting higher rates of plant growth, while the Haitian side is drier with less arable land. But, "while those environmental differences did contribute to the different economic trajectories of the two countries, a larger part of the explanation involved social and political differences, of which there were many that penalized the Haitian economy relative to the Dominican economy."

Many of Haiti's problems are a legacy from its status as a former colony of France, which developed a slave-based plantation agriculture in Haiti to suit its own ends. As a result, Haiti is far more densely populated than its counterpart, which has contributed to a much higher rate of deforestation. Also, because Haiti was a plantation-style economy, it did not develop trading relations to the extent its Dominican counterpart did. This has been an important difference because the leaders of the Dominican Republic sought to develop a modern economy and industrialize their country as a way of profiting themselves, while, historically, Haitian leaders have been content to extract wealth from peasants and the underclass in their plantation style economy.

Both Haiti and the Dominican Republic have suffered under despotic leaderships. Ironically, however, Dominican despots have had a far better record in managing their natural resources – and in particular extending protections to their natural forests – than their Haitian counterparts. Indeed, the Dominican Republic has been fortunate in having a strong tradition of grassroots ecological awareness – i.e., bottom-up management – coupled with a strong-armed, top-down ecological management. The leaders of the Dominican Republic may have had their own agenda in protecting the country's forests – to prevent rivals with competing logging operations – or they may have been environmentally earnest. But whatever the reason, the Dominican Republic is at least holding its own with its environmental challenges, while Haiti is a poor country becoming poorer and more desperate as time goes by.

CHINA, THE LURCHING GIANT

"China is the world's most populous country, with about 1,300,000,000 people, or one-fifth of the world's total." The third largest country in terms of area, China already has a huge economy and its economic growth rate is the fastest of any major country – about 10% per annum, which is quadruple the growth rate of most First World economies. China is an industrial powerhouse, but it also has some of the biggest environmental problems of any major industrial country and these challenges are only getting worse. These problems include air pollution, soil erosion, disappearing wetlands, desertification, biodiversity loss, water pollution, invasive species, salinization and numerous others. These problems are causing enormous economic losses, health problems and social conflict within China. But because of China's size and importance, its problems will inevitably spill over to the rest of the world.

China is already one of the world's largest contributors of pollutants and ozone-depleting substances, but it is also one of the world's largest importers of timber from tropical rainforests, thus making it a major force for global deforestation. China, like many other developing countries that aspire to a First World lifestyle, presents a difficult conundrum: can the planet sustain so many people at a First World level of consumption and impact?

Recognizing its own population problem, China has instituted mandatory fertility control - a one child per couple policy - that has limited the population growth rate to 1.3%. Though considered Draconian by Western standards, China's fertility policy is almost certainly necessary to avert famine, a decreased standard of living associated with severe over-population and natural catastrophes induced by the demands the Chinese population makes on its environment.

The Chinese government has had a mixed record on environmental matters. On the one hand, there is a record of substantial corruption, disastrous economic and ecological policies – encouraged in the past by the misguided conviction that only Capitalist countries caused ecological damage – and the fact that China lacks energy efficient means of production and relies heavily on inefficient fossil fuels like coal. On the other hand, China's top-down management has shown it can quickly implement difficult, but necessary measures to deal with impending crisis, as they did with their family planning policies. The

conundrum, however, is that as long as present circum-
stances remain, the world can hardly sustain China, other
third world countries and current First World countries, all
living at First World levels simultaneously.

"MINING" AUSTRALIA

"Mining in the literal sense – i.e., coal, iron, and so on – is
a key component of Australia's economy today." But there
is another sense, a metaphorical sense, in which "mining"
has been a part of Australia's environmental history and
much of its ecological problems today. That's because
"mining," when you get down to it, is the extraction of
non-renewable resources (coal doesn't renew itself the
way forests do). But Australia has managed to treat its
renewable resources – forests, fish and topsoil – as if
they could be exploited indefinitely, which they can't, with
devastating results.

Australia presents an especially interesting case study
because its problems may provide a foretaste for the
problems likely to face much of the First World in the
future if present trends continue. To begin with, despite
its reputation as lush and pristine, Australia actually
has an exceptionally fragile environment. Much of the
damage has been man made and conservative cultural
attitudes – "this is my land, no one can tell me what I may
do with it" – continue to provide obstacles to crucial re-

forms, particularly water management policies. Without such reforms, it is likely that Australians will experience a steadily deteriorating environment and quality of life.

Fortunately, Australia has an educated population and there are signs that cultural attitudes are shifting in the direction of environmental concern. In particular, peer pressure among farmers is encouraging agricultural practices that are more sustainable because farmers have begun to realize their way of life, and that of their descendants, is threatened unless they make changes. And, Australian economists and government officials have begun to reconsider the wisdom of many agricultural subsidies that have encouraged destructive farming policies.

Will Australia adopt much needed reforms in time? Because Australia is a First World country, a complete overnight collapse — as happened on Easter Island, for instance — is unlikely. Rather, a slow, but irreversible decline in living standards is likely absent dramatic reforms. In many ways, Australia's predicament is our own.

LESSONS

Why do societies fail to anticipate or respond to environmental crises? One reason groups do disastrous things is that they have no prior experience of the problems they encounter. British colonists, for example, who introduced foxes and rabbits to Australia, had no idea that these species alien to Australia would have such a devastating impact on Australia's native vegetation.

Ignorance can take many forms, including failing to learn lessons from one's ancestors - a particular problem in preliterate societies - or a voluntary forgetfulness (i.e., Americans buying gas guzzling cars soon after the 1974 Gulf oil crisis). But perhaps the most common way societies fail to understand a problem is when a slow trend is concealed by wide up-and-down variations. "Politicians," for example, "use the term 'creeping normalcy' to refer to such slow trends concealed within noisy fluctuations," as when citizens fail to notice traffic congestion is mostly getting worse over successive years. Global warming is certainly another case in point. "Landscape amnesia" is another term related to "creeping normalcy," and it refers to changes in a given environment so gradual that not even local inhabitants view the changes occurring as anything but normal.

Societies can also recognize environmental problems, but fail to do anything about them. One of the most common reasons this occurs is that frequently some sort of practice is "rational bad behavior" – behavior that is, "good for some group, but bad for everyone else." For instance, without effective regulations to protect a communally owned resource such as fishing grounds, over-fishing could quickly deplete that resource. Yet until such regulations exist, each individual fisherman will reason, "If I don't catch the fish myself, someone else will."

Governments can devise solutions to the "tragedy of the commons" described above, but so can consumers. Consumer boycotts and environmental seals of approval can encourage companies to conduct themselves in an environmentally friendly manner. Additionally, many oil companies have found it is in their long-term interests to avoid the high clean-up costs associated with toxic oil spills and that they are more likely to attract business if they project an environmentally friendly image. Of course, consumers need to recognize their common interest in preserving increasingly scarce resources and adhere to more sustainable levels of consumption.

Other impediments to solving environmental problems exist. Often political elites benefit from destructive practices and are able to insulate themselves from accountability for the damage they do to the common good. And not infrequently, deeply held religious beliefs actually encourage disastrous practices. But even when society correctly perceives its problems, the solutions it implements may be too little too late and it may end up backfiring, or the environmental problem may be too formidable even to be solved.

CONCLUSION

As a species we are:

- Destroying natural habitats at an accelerating rate.
- Losing biodiversity.
- Suffering increasing soil erosion rates.
- Depleting the world's inexpensively available energy sources (oil, natural gas, and coal).
- Generating record levels of toxic chemicals.
- Damaging the protective ozone layer by the use of greenhouse gases.
- And making more demands on the world's resources through population growth.

Current trends put us on a perilous course. However, there are reasons for optimism. Technology is often a double-edged sword, so we cannot expect scientific or technological breakthroughs to solve our problems. Nor will our problems solve themselves. But although we face serious risks, the challenges we face are not entirely out of our control. The U.S. government, for example, has taken courageous actions in the past to reduce the levels of six major pollutants over the last 30 years, even as energy consumption and population increased. What is needed is the recognition that bold, courageous and anticipatory decisions are needed before problems reach a crisis stage. In our globalized, interconnected world, environmental problems will tend to be magnified, effecting us all. But globalization also has an upside; we have the ability to learn from mistakes past, share information and respond to challenges in ways that past societies never could.

ABOUT THE SUMMARY PUBLISHER

The content of this book is owned by CapitolReader, a publisher dedicated to bringing you executive summaries of the best political books. These book summaries allow you to read the key points and arguments being made by political leaders, satirists, pundits and journalists.

This is a nonpartisan service, and throughout our publication cycle summaries are alternated by party affiliation. The summaries do not offer judgment or opinion on the content of each book. Instead, the ideas, viewpoints and arguments are presented just as the author has intended.

45511871R00020

Made in the USA
Middletown, DE
17 May 2019